MW01029175

To:_____

From:_____

God Is
With You
Wherever
You Go

52 devotions

TRAVEL
Devotional

BroadStreet
PUBLISHING

BroadStreet Publishing Group LLC
Racine, Wisconsin, USA
Broadstreetpublishing.com

God Is With You Wherever You Go:
Travel Devotional

ISBN 978-1-4245-4997-9

Devotional entries composed by Vicki Kuyper.

Design by Chris Garborg | www.garborgdesign.com
Editorial services by Michelle Winger | www.literallyprecise.com

Printed in China.

15   16   17   18   19   20   21   7   6   5   4   3   2   1

Welcome to Adventure!

You're about to embark on a journey to...somewhere. Did you know the word *journey* comes from the French word *jour*, which means "day"? Each new day holds a unique adventure. A *jour*nal is a record of where each day leads.

Unlike a traditional travel journal that provides you with space to record what happens during your trip, this travel devotional offers you some spiritual food for thought. Each travel-themed devotional can stand on its own, so you can use this journal on multiple adventures, from a weekend road trip to the trip of a lifetime.

At the end of each devotional entry, you'll find a page with a question or action step to help you personalize what you've read. You can use the space below to respond to what God's teaching you, as a prayer journal, or as a travel diary of what you see and do each day. It's up to you!

Just remember, wherever you go, you never travel alone. God is with you every step of the way.

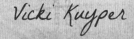

Vicki Kuyper

Packing a Sense of Purpose

By faith Abraham, when called to go
to a place he would later receive as
his inheritance, obeyed and went,
even though he did not know where
he was going (Hebrews 11:8, NIV).

When we set off on a journey, we generally have a plan.
Before getting into the car or boarding the plane, we've
spent time budgeting, packing, and making reservations.
We know what time we'll leave, what route we'll take,
and when we're due to arrive. Most importantly, we know
where we're headed. After all, our destination is the
point of the whole trip, right? But what if it's not? What
if it's not how seeing the world changes *us*, but how our
presence changes *the world*?

Over and over again we've heard that God has a purpose
for our lives. That includes the days we spend on vacation.

Often these are me-time days, when our goal is to relax, be entertained, blow our diets, and sleep in late. Yes, we may schedule in time to exercise, but even that is because we want to take better care of ourselves.

If God's ultimate purpose is that we love him and love others, we need to temper our *me* time with *we* time. And that extends further than just to the friends and family who may be traveling with us. This doesn't mean we have to volunteer to work in a soup kitchen while we're celebrating our anniversary in Paris. It simply means that we'll be more intentional about keeping our hearts open, as well as our eyes. We'll treat the people we meet with respect, kindness, and an awareness of how precious they are in God's sight. This includes those who wait on us, clean our hotel rooms, and even those who cut in front of us in the buffet line.

We may believe the purpose of our vacation is to spend time with the kids and see the world, but God may have an even richer purpose in mind. If we're open to the gentle nudge of his Spirit, he may lead us on an adventure we didn't see coming. One chance encounter, one gesture of kindness or insightful word could help move someone closer toward the open arms of a waiting God.

Today, try to see each person who crosses your path from God's point of view. He knows their names, even if you don't.

Are We There Yet?

Don't be pulled in different directions
or worried about a thing. Be
saturated in prayer throughout
each day, offering your faith-filled
requests before God with overflowing
gratitude. Tell him every detail of
your life (Philippians 4:6, TPT).

Often the most dreaded part of vacation, other than
dealing with all of the dirty laundry we face when we
return home, is getting to wherever we want to go.
Gone are the days when traveling by planes, trains, and
automobiles was a celebrated part of our journey. Now
it's simply a means to an end.

Long hours squished into cramped quarters shared with
snarky fellow-travelers isn't a relaxing scenario. But
expecting the worst doesn't help us feel any more at ease.
That's why it's important to adjust our attitude—right
along with our seat—the minute we hit the road. After all,

a vacation is not just a destination. It includes a journey. We can't travel without moving!

As you pull away from home, remind yourself, "*Now* is when my adventure begins." Picture leaving anything you're struggling with or anxious about right there on the curb. Then, do something risky. Ask God to replace what you've left behind with two gifts you'll need to pack for the road ahead: patience and a sense of humor. What's risky about asking for them is you'll undoubtedly be given the opportunity to use them. (On the flip side, you'll also have more amusing anecdotes to share when you return home!)

Until teleportation becomes a viable vacation option, the journeys we make will take time. Why waste it? Exploration and relaxation can begin right now. Instead of checking your phone, check out the view along the way. Rediscover the joy of people watching, playing license plate bingo, or seeing what shapes you can find in the clouds. Refuse to let other people's anxiety or frustration become your own. Hold tightly to patience and humor— and enjoy the ride.

Transportation is part of every vacation. Every time you buckle up, remember to secure patience and a sense of adventure right along with you.

The Perfect Souvenir

> "You are a holy people, who belong to the LORD your God. Of all the people on earth, the LORD your God has chosen you to be his own special treasure" (Deuteronomy 7:6, NLT).

Cowboy boots from Texas. Turkish delight from Istanbul. A cheesehead hat from Wisconsin. Wooden shoes from Amsterdam. We love bringing home a little something from vacation. It's proof we've actually gone somewhere and done something out of the ordinary. Because once we get home, our lives quickly go back to normal and our recent vacation can almost seem like a mirage.

Souvenirs can be tangible touchstones to happy memories. They can also be a total waste of time and money. Before you spend your hard-earned cash on a vacation-themed trinket for yourself or someone else, carefully consider why you're tempted to purchase that

Eiffel Tower snow globe. Instant gratification may feel great in the moment, but our impulse buys often have a very short shelf life. Need proof? Visit any second-hand store or charity drop box.

Emotion can lead us to buy things we don't need—or even want. Cramming a kitschy keepsake into our carry-on luggage won't make a vacation last any longer. Perhaps those dollars, euros, or pesos would be better spent by saving them for a return trip!

When Jesus' long-distance trip from heaven to earth was coming to an end, he didn't hurry out and pick up a little something to carry back to heaven with him. He was more concerned with the welfare of something that has an eternal shelf life: you. People were the sole purpose of Jesus' journey. He wasn't here on a vacation. He was here on a mission of mercy.

You're not a trinket to Jesus. You're a treasure—one he looks forward to bringing home with him one day. Until then, celebrate the people and places you have the opportunity to experience here on earth. Happy memories are a great souvenir. They're free, easy to carry, and never need dusting.

Is there a souvenir you'd really like to bring home from this trip? If so, consider what it really represents to you.

I Need a Vacation

On the seventh day God had finished
his work of creation, so he rested
from all his work (Genesis 2:2, NLT).

God knows when to take a break. After creating the world,
he scheduled a day off. After ministering to demanding
crowds, Jesus headed to a solitary place. After hearing his
friend John the Baptist had been beheaded, our Savior
took some time by himself to grieve. Often, we're not
quite as wise.

We push ourselves to the limit and beyond. We work
nights, weekends, and can't seem to turn off our brains
when we get into bed. We check our email at the dinner
table, at stop lights, and when we lose interest in the
conversation at social occasions. We only schedule
time off because if we don't use it, we'll lose it. Even on
vacation, we never totally disconnect from what's going
on back home—whether at the office or through social

media. We get in the habit of believing that we're not only indispensable, we're indestructible.

Enjoying a little R & R is not a waste of time. It's one way of following God's own example. When Jesus was physically and emotionally spent, he didn't head off in search of a beach chair and a fruity drink with an umbrella in it. He found a quiet place to pray.

If you're on a family vacation, finding a quiet place to spend time with your heavenly Father may feel like a challenge. Get creative: head to the balcony, take a bubble bath, go for a walk. If the kids are with you, linger a bit as you bring up the rear. Call a family silence summit where you all sit quietly for a predetermined amount of time and look closely at what's around you. Afterwards, take turns sharing your favorite part of the scene. You can use the time as your own personal worship service.

Reconnecting with God through prayer will help you relax mentally, physically, and spiritually. But to reconnect, you first have to disconnect. Turn off your phone and power down your computer. Try plugging yourself into the ultimate power source while on vacation. It's a great way to recharge from the inside out.

If God were sitting across from you right now, what would you say to him? Go ahead. He's there—and that's prayer.

Worship through a Lens

The earth is the LORD's, and
everything in it,
the world, and all who live in it
(Psalm 24:1, NIV).

The Hallelujah Chorus, a whispered prayer, the click of
a shutter...these can all be forms of praise. We may not
be accustomed to thinking of photography as a form
of worship, but consider what motivates us to try and
capture the scene before us via digital film. Awe. Joy.
Wonder. Beauty. Love. We want to remember, and share
with others, something that has moved us. More often
than not, whatever moved us emotionally was created or
inspired by the hand of God.

Not every photograph is praise materialized. Sometimes—
especially on vacation—we mindlessly snap away with
our camera phone or point-and-shoot out of habit. After

all, today is not just your ordinary day! We are seeing things we may never have the opportunity to experience again. So we point, shoot, and don't really stop to savor what's right in front of us because we feel we've captured it digitally. We'll save it so we can look at it later, when we have time. Or until there are so many images on our phone that we have to delete them to make room for a software upgrade.

It's time to sharpen your focus. Start by becoming more aware of what is in front of your lens. Why are you inspired to capture this image? Thank God for his part in its creation or its creator. Imagine every image you take as a thank-you postcard to God. Not only will you find a unique way to spend more time interacting with your heavenly Father, you'll also find your inner well of gratitude overflowing more regularly. That makes any vacation day more enjoyable.

An added bonus is that you'll take more thoughtful, less random, photos. For that, your friends and family back home (not to mention those on social media), will thank you.

Today, before every photo you take,
thank God for what you see in the frame.

The "Up" Side of Jet Lag

Then you will go on your way in safety,
and your foot will not stumble.
When you lie down, you will not be afraid;
when you lie down, your sleep will be
sweet (Proverbs 3:23-24, NIV).

There's nothing like trying to sleep on a plane that
makes you appreciate the comfort of your very own bed.
Headphones, a slumber mask, a neck pillow, a blanket as
thin as a single ply tissue...they're all feeble attempts to
try and trick us into believing it is bedtime. But our bodies
know better.

Even crossing a single time zone by plane, train, or
automobile can mess with our sleep cycle. The more time
zones we cross, the messier things can get. If we have the
privilege of flying far enough away to experience jet lag,

it can leave us feeling groggy, grumpy, and anxious about waking up in the middle of the night.

There are things to do to minimize jet lag's effects. Leave well-rested. Don't save packing and planning for the evening before you board the plane. Change your watch. Don't keep reminding yourself what time it is at home. When you arrive at your destination, head out for a good walk in the sunshine. Try to stay awake until a reasonable bedtime. Then, lay back and let those droopy eyelids finally close.

If you're wide awake at 2 a.m., what then? Consider it a wake-up call from God. After all, he's the one who designed our circadian rhythm and need for sleep. God knows us so well. If he didn't provide us with a built-in sleep mode, we'd probably keep going and going and going. Instead, God established an 8-hour mandatory vacation for each of us every day.

Instead of tossing and turning when you can't sleep, tell God how thankful you are for the way he made you—and for the gift of sleep. But don't stop there. Keep the list going. Thank him for everything that comes to mind until you finally drift back to sleep. Don't worry about nodding off mid-conversation. You can pick up where you left off anytime, anywhere. There will always be more to say.

If you have trouble sleeping
on vacation, try counting your
blessings instead of sheep.

Become a Student of the World

Do yourself a favor and love wisdom.
Learn all you can,
Then watch your life flourish and
prosper! (Proverbs 19:8, TPT)

Until time travel becomes reality, museums are one of the only ways we can actually step back into the past. The Resistance Museum in Amsterdam challenges us to ask ourselves what we would have done if faced with the atrocities of World War II. Cleveland's Rock and Roll Hall of Fame transports us back to the day we first heard Elvis, Louis Armstrong, or the Beatles.

There are museums that celebrate different cultures, display priceless artwork, inform us about natural history, and even teach us more than we ever wanted to know about a particular subject. Case in point: the Instant Ramen Museum in Osaka, Japan, and the International

Toilet Museum in New Delhi, India. Who knows what we can learn when we're on the road?

For some of us, visiting a museum feels like being sent back to school—when we're supposed to be on vacation! But learning is not at odds with relaxation. It can actually spark new interests, challenge us to rethink long-held opinions, and stir up some interesting conversations with our traveling companions. In other words, it can help us *grow*. If we long to return from vacation feeling like a new man or a new woman, this is one way we can do exactly that.

But it takes more than viewing artifacts and taking in information to change us. We need to put what we learn into context. We need to ask ourselves, *Is there any lesson I can apply from what I've seen today?*

It's been said that those who don't learn from history are doomed to repeat it. Why do you think the Bible includes books like Exodus, Chronicles, and Acts? Life is too short to learn every lesson we need to know through firsthand experience. We can learn from the victories and mistakes of others.

When we apply what we've learned in a way that draws us closer to becoming who God's created us to be, we grow in wisdom as well as maturity. When on vacation, a trip to a museum can help move us a little further down that road.

If possible, visit a museum on this trip. Share one lesson you learn with your traveling companions.

_____

_____

_____

_____

_____

_____

_____

_____

_____

_____

Lost in a Foreign Land

"The Son of Man came to seek and to save the lost" (Luke 19:10, ESV).

Lost is not a word we like to use on vacation. We don't want to lose our passport, a good night's sleep, or our way. When we travel somewhere for the first time, we're entering foreign territory—even if we don't cross international borders.

In some respects, the novelty of an unfamiliar locale is one of the things we like best about it. We want to experience something we've never seen or done before, to expand our horizons both literally and figuratively. But entering unexplored territory carries with it an element of risk. It's easy to get turned around in an unfamiliar city, especially if we don't speak the language.

While it's true that a little research and planning beforehand can help us gain our bearings more quickly, the easiest way to relax and enjoy our new surroundings is to put ourselves in the hands of a local guide. A qualified guide knows the culture, the language, and the lay of the land. He or she also knows the sights we don't want to miss and the pitfalls we should avoid.

It's one thing to talk about being lost in a foreign land. It's quite another to talk about being *lost* in light of Scripture. We don't usually picture the people Jesus referred to as "the lost" as tourists wandering in confusion around an unfamiliar city. But maybe we should.

At heart, each and every one of us is a pilgrim searching for the road home. We're all in need of a knowledgeable guide to help us navigate the twists and turns of life. With Jesus as our guide, and God's Word as our map, we can figure out the direction we should go today—at least spiritually…geographically? Well, that's another story.

Today, if you encounter people whose culture or religious beliefs differ from your own, remind yourself that they are fellow pilgrims. How does this affect the way you view them?

_____

_____

_____

_____

_____

_____

_____

_____

_____

_____

_____

_____

Traveling Companions

Two people are better off than one,
for they can help each other succeed.
If one person falls, the other can
reach out and help. But someone
who falls alone is in real trouble
(Ecclesiastes 4:9–10, NLT).

Mark Twain said, "I have found out that there ain't no surer way to find out whether you like people or hate them than to travel with them." Anyone who's taken a trip that ignited a few relational sparks along the way knows the truth behind those words. High expectations, tight budgets, close quarters, and a break from our regular routine can leave us all a bit testy. And, unfortunately, those closest to us are usually the ones we are least concerned about offending.

It's easy to focus our attention on that certain someone who happens to be getting on our last nerve. This may be the first time we've noticed quirky idiosyncrasies or personal grooming habits that leave us rolling our eyes. Before we start ranting, whether inside our head or behind that person's back, let's take a good look at ourselves. After all, we are the only people we can actually change.

No one can ruin our vacation without our permission. Before hard feelings become carved in stone, spend some time with God asking him to reveal your own part in the situation. If you believe there's a real problem, be honest enough to bring it out into the open. Don't stuff it until after the vacation ends—because like the pile of dirty laundry in your suitcase, it will grow. Speak your mind; but be kind.

In the long run, relationships are more valuable than checking something off our bucket list. More often than not, they're also the actual highlight of the trip. Seeing the Great Wall of China can be awe-inspiring, but how much more wonderful it is to be able to share that experience with someone who's close to your heart.

Each morning, pray for your traveling
companions. Ask God to help you
better see each person as a unique
asset to the memorable day ahead.

Say "No" to Boredom

> He counts the number of the stars;
> He calls them all by name
> (Psalm 147:4, NKJV).

Our world is so big that even if we traveled every day of our lives we'd never see it all. There would still be lagoons to snorkel, mountains to crest, and hidden nooks and crannies of creation to explore. Yet consider how small our home planet is compared with the whole of God's creation. Earth is merely a grain of sand on the shore of a limitless universe.

Still, we get bored. Once something, or somewhere, that was new becomes familiar to us, we lose that initial sense of wonder and fascination. We stop really looking because we believe we've seen it all, but we still crave that first taste of discovery. That rush of excitement and awe. So we plan our next vacation, hoping to recapture that initial thrill by journeying to somewhere new.

It has been said that the real voyage of discovery consists not in seeking new landscapes, but in having new eyes (Marcel Proust). Even our backyard holds hidden mysteries. We simply stop exploring because we believe we've already conquered this tiny corner of the universe. But right under our nose there are buds beginning to bloom, leaves preparing to fall, lizards scurrying over rocks, or tiny ants carrying tremendous loads. Above us there's a sky filled with so many distant worlds that our minds cannot fathom its expanse.

Today, wherever the road takes you, open your eyes. Instead of hurrying past what you've already seen, look again. Take time to appreciate the detail God has woven into nature. Look at the faces of the people you pass along the street. Notice the buildings, the food, the artwork, the amazing innovation and imagination that originated from the human brain—another of God's masterworks.

Just say no to boredom. Nurture curiosity instead of apathy. You don't have to stop exploring—even if you never journey far from home.

The next time you find yourself edging toward boredom, replace it with curiosity. Explore. Take a closer look. Ask questions. Thank God for the amazing things you see.

Traveling Mercies

The steadfast love of the LORD never
ceases;
his mercies never come to an end;
they are new every morning;
great is your faithfulness
(Lamentations 3:22-23, ESV).

Praying for *traveling mercies* is kind of a secret code
phrase we often use when we're talking to God about an
upcoming journey. At its heart, what we're really saying
is, "Please keep us safe. We're heading out of our comfort
zone and we feel less in control than we usually do. So,
pretty please, don't let anything mess up our plans."

If we're honest with ourselves, asking for traveling mercies
is pretty much in line with how we pray most of the time.
We come to God with a Burger King Customer mentality.
We put in an order for life *our* way, and we expect God to
be prompt in serving up what we've asked.

Of course, Jesus did the same thing. When faced with death on the cross, he prayed, "If it is possible, let this cup of suffering be taken away from me" (Matthew 26:39, NLT). But then, Jesus turned that prayer around by adding, "Yet I want your will to be done, not mine."

Whether we're on the road, or safe at home, putting God's will before our own is what keeps our prayer requests in their proper place. It also reminds us who is actually in control at all times.

We need true traveling mercies every day of our lives. Mercy is compassion extended by someone who is in a position to cause harm to someone else. Yikes. That sounds pretty scary—and a God as mighty as ours without mercy *would* be scary.

It's true that God is big and powerful, while we are small and relatively powerless. But we are loved. Immeasurably. Unconditionally. Eternally. That means we can trust our mighty God enough to say, "Have it your way," anytime, anywhere.

Consider why you may be hesitant to say "Have it your way" to God on vacation. Talk to him about your hopes and fears.

Behind the Words

> At one time all the people of the
> world spoke the same language and
> used the same words
> (Genesis 11:1, NLT).

There's nothing like traveling to a foreign country to make us wish the builders of the Tower of Babel hadn't needed a good dose of humility delivered by the hand of God. Imagine how easy it would be if everyone spoke the same language? *Thank you* would be *thank you* everywhere we went instead of *grazie, merci, danke, obrigado, gracias* and on and on and on.

Conversation is difficult enough without a language barrier. How many times have your words been misunderstood when you thought you'd made yourself perfectly clear? Language is tricky, even if everyone involved in the conversation is speaking the same one.

But words are not the only way we communicate. We send a message to those around us via the way we treat them. Kindness, respect, eye contact, a warm smile... there are so many ways to connect with others that do not involve words. When we find ourselves in a situation where words don't work, we need to rely more than ever on communicating a message of congeniality and consideration.

One way to do that is to try to learn a few useful phrases in the local language before we land on foreign soil, familiarize ourselves with local customs and currency, know what traditional dishes we can expect on a menu, and dress appropriately for the culture we're visiting.

When we travel, we are guests. Let's be guests others would be excited to invite back, instead of those who wind up as fodder for "you won't believe what those crazy tourists did today" stories. Making friends while we're making memories (even if we never understand a word the other person says) makes every journey a more enjoyable one.

Today, pay attention to the ways you communicate without words. Do you project more positive or negative nonverbal messages?

A Hush amid the Hurry

Be still, and know that I am God;
I will be exalted among the nations,
I will be exalted in the earth!
(Psalm 46:10, NKJV)

When we're traveling, life can feel as though it's stuck
on fast-forward. There's so much to see and so little time
to do it! If we've traveled a long distance, we're fully
aware that we may never pass this way again, so we
don't want to miss a thing. We fill our waking hours with
sightseeing—crossing landmarks off our list like groceries
at the supermarket. If we're vacationing with the family,
we work hard to keep the kids entertained and the
activities rolling. But there's a need for silence amidst the
wonderful chaos we've scheduled into our vacation time.
Moments where we just sit and *be*.

If we're uncomfortable with silence at home, chances are we won't feel any differently on vacation. However, there's no better time than today to begin a practice that not only helps us enjoy the beauty of this very moment but invites us to draw closer to God at the same time. We can practice it anytime, anywhere. What better time could there be than on vacation when our senses are already attuned to make the most of every moment?

Find a comfortable spot and sit: mouth closed, eyes and ears open. Then pay attention. Instead of diligently trying to capture the beauty of a sunset on your camera phone, sit in silence and observe the show from start to finish. Or find a comfortable bench any time of day. Sit down and close your eyes. Listen to the sound of the waves, the rise and fall of birdsong, or the musicality of people speaking a language you can't understand.

After your heart and mind have quieted down enough to hear what's really going on around you, tell God, "I'm here." Rest in the assurance that he is there as well. Listen for what God has to say to you in the spaces between activities, when you're quiet enough to hear his voice. Be still, and let him show you just how big he is and what a wonderful world he's made.

For at least five minutes each day while you're on vacation, find a place to be still, soak in your surroundings, and listen for God's voice.

What Is It?

"Give us this day our daily bread"
(Matthew 6:11, NKJV).

As the Israelites began their forty-year journey of wandering through the desert, they grumbled about a lot of things. One of them was their lack of food. So, God provided. Each morning the ground was covered with a flaky, white substance the Israelites used to bake into bread. They called it manna, which means *what is it?*

When we're far from home, we may find ourselves asking the same question when an unfamiliar dish is placed in front of us at mealtime. Whether it's lefse, papadums, tortillas, arepa, brioche, chapati, focaccia, bagels, or baguettes, our daily bread looks and tastes distinctively different depending on where we are in the world. Sometimes, sampling local cuisine becomes one of our favorite memories of the trip. Other times, it literally leaves a bad taste in our mouths.

Regardless of whether we can't get enough of the local delicacies or they leave us reaching for our antacids, chances are we will not go hungry. If we can afford to take a vacation, we can afford to eat during the trip. We may have to pinch pennies, pack lunches, and snub restaurants with stars attached to their names—or not. Either way, we will eat. And that is reason to be thankful.

The tradition of saying a blessing around the table reminds us of that fact. Having enough to eat—or more than enough—is not a given. It is a gift. Taking time to thank God for what's on our plate—whether it's samosas, kimchi, or pickled pigs' feet—reminds us that food is first and foremost fuel. It's what keeps our bodies moving. Taste is an added bonus. It doesn't make the food any more beneficial to us, simply more pleasurable.

Savor every bite you take today. Eat slowly. Really taste what's on your plate. Thank God for his provision of food as well as for the person who prepared it even if you're tempted to nickname it *manna*.

Whatever you find on your plate today, thank God for it—not by reciting a rote blessing, but by telling him honestly how much you appreciate his gift of more than just daily bread.

Between Heaven and the Deep Blue Sea

> Let the sea and everything in it
> shout his praise!
> Let the earth and all living things
> join in (Psalm 98:7, NLT).

Not every journey leads to the sea, but with the ocean covering more than 70% of our planet, chances are good that we'll fly over it, sail on it, dive beneath it, or lounge beside it at least once during our lifetime. Even once is enough to leave a permanent impression.

Its moods are as profound as its mystery. One minute it's as calm as a shallow pond. The next, its surface roils like water in a teakettle, set to boil. Waves crash and tides turn, casting briny treasures up onto the shore. Seashells, starfish, and clumps of kelp provide just a glimpse of what lies beneath—evidence of a fantastically foreign world. It's a world so unlike the one in which we were designed to live that if we care to pay it a visit, we're unable to move, or even breathe, without making some major adjustments.

In some ways, the ocean is a bit like heaven. It's as close as our last breath, but it's impossible for us to explore without undergoing a physical change. It's a foreign land and our true home at the same time. Though we've read bits and pieces about it in the Bible, so much remains a mystery. Mansions, streets of gold, crowns we cast at Jesus' feet, eternal life, no more tears...what is literal and what is a metaphor? Certainly our limited language can't help but fail when it comes to accurately describing a world where God dwells in all his glory.

Like the deepest depths of the sea, heaven's borders are beyond our grasp right now. We can only travel there through conjecture and imagination. But Jesus has assured us that one day we'll make that journey. We'll experience firsthand what God has prepared for us. That day could be ten, twenty, or fifty years from now. Or it could be tomorrow.

Until then, listen to the waves, take deep breaths of the salty sea air, and pick up a shell along the shore. Allow the ocean to become a touchstone to heaven for you—a reminder that there's so much more to this life than what we can see with our eyes.

Take a few moments to consider what you believe about heaven. What, or who, helped you form these beliefs? Talk to God about your hopes and fears about traveling to your future home.

Sunrise, Sunset

The God of gods, the mighty Lord
himself, has spoken!
He shouts out over all the people of
the earth,
In every brilliant sunrise and every
beautiful sunset, saying,
"Listen to me!" (Psalm 50:1, TPT)

Leave it to an artist to begin and end each day with a
masterpiece. At sunrise and sunset, God paints the sky
with color, light, and creativity. Some days carry a more
subtle light show than others, but all are worthy of notice.
Each momentary display happens only once in the history
of time and differs depending where in the world we're
viewing it from.

The fact that the sun rises and sets every single day lulls
us into the mistaken belief that nothing extraordinary
is taking place. Unless the entire sky looks like a raging
wildfire, we rarely stop what we're doing and take note.

Even then, we may snap a quick photo to post online or admire later instead of enjoying it here and now.

Vacations are different. We break our routine. We expect to see and do things that are out of the ordinary—at least for us. So why not make time to enjoy sunrises and sunsets? Sure, sleeping in is one of the perks of vacation days. But why not choose one morning to wake before dawn and witness the first light of day? Sit quietly with God and tell him what you think of his handiwork and how much you're looking forward to the day ahead. You may find those few quiet moments of contemplation and praise are the highlight of your day.

Then, do the same thing for sunset. Choose one night when the timing is right for you to watch God's light show from beginning to end. Quiet your heart and your thoughts and simply enjoy what you see. Reflect on where today has taken you—the highs and the lows. Then, listen for the whisper of God's voice in the stillness.

We can't slow down time, but we can make the most of it. By stopping long enough to appreciate the sunrise and sunset, we become more aware of how each day is a little life, bracketed by beauty—whether we're on vacation or not.

At sunrise or sunset, write your own psalm of thanks to God.

Play Time

I lie awake at night thinking of you—
of how much you have helped me—
and how I rejoice through the night
beneath the protecting shadow of
your wings (Psalm 63:6-7, TLB).

We couldn't help but watch the clock. As the minutes counted down on the last day of school, we knew that once that bell rang, we were free! Free to play, to hang out with our friends, or maybe take a trip with our family. Summer vacation stretched out in front of us like an unexplored fantasy land. For the next few months, anything was possible.

Then we grew up. Grocery shopping, mortgages, deadlines, cholesterol levels, and families of our own filled our days—and our thoughts. And even when it came time for vacation, all too often we packed everything that was mentally weighing us down right along with our swimsuit and clean underwear. We may have taken vacation days, but they weren't anything like those summer days we enjoyed as a child.

They can be. Play time is as important for adults as it is for kids. We need time to laugh, to explore, to create, to try new things, to dream. We need to give ourselves permission to allow the child in us to come out and play.

To do that, we need to let go of our fear of what others may think. We may look silly having an imaginary tea party with our grandkids. We may fail the first time we try paddle boarding. We may skin our knees sliding into home plate. But if we're fully engaged in what we're doing, we'll not only rediscover how *fun* fun can be, we'll momentarily forget all of the tough stuff that may be waiting for us at home.

So, go ahead. Wear that swimsuit in public even if you're not a size two. Play a game of Ping-Pong even if it's been decades since you held a paddle in your hands. Sing songs around the campfire even if you can't carry a tune. Wear a silly hat to a theme park just because you can. Try to see the world around you through the eyes of a child. Then, go out and play.

Consider what your expectations of this vacation day would be if you were a child, instead of an adult. Do you see any opportunities for play? Take one and see what happens.

Picture Perfect Days

> Farmers who wait for perfect
> weather never plant.
> If they watch every cloud, they never
> harvest (Ecclesiastes 11:4, NLT).

James Whitcomb Riley wrote, "It's no use to grumble and complain; it's just as cheap and easy to rejoice; when God sorts out the weather and sends rain—why, rain's my choice." Chances are that Mr. Riley was not on vacation when he wrote those words.

Though our heads may fully agree with Mr. Riley's sentiment, our hearts may not fare as well when torrential rain washes out our week at the beach or unseasonably warm weather turns our ski weekend into a slush fest. That's because in the vacation of our dreams, every day is picture perfect, suitable to the activities we have planned. Our vacation dreams don't always come true. Hurricanes, blizzards, and heat waves pay little mind to our travel schedule.

That's why it's good to have a Plan B. Before you leave on vacation, do a little research. Find some indoor activities close to where you're going to stay. See if there's a movie theater, bowling alley, or museum nearby. Take a jigsaw puzzle, a board game, or a few of your favorite DVDs zipped into an easy-to-pack plastic bag. Throw a rain poncho or umbrella into your luggage just in case. Then, all that's left to do is go with the flow.

As Mr. Riley wisely noted, grumbling and complaining won't change a thing—except perhaps turn a good mood into a bad one. And a bad mood can suck the joy out of a vacation day even more readily than adverse weather.

Expect the best, pack for the worst, and prepare to make some unexpected memories along the way. The beautiful world God has given us needs all kind of weather to keep the crops growing, the animals breeding, and the fresh water flowing. Your bad weather may be someone else's answer to prayer.

When you awake to good weather on your vacation, take a moment to thank God for it. If adverse weather comes your way, consider what is good about it. Then, thank God just the same.

Someone Else's Shoes

> You saw me before I was born.
> Every day of my life was recorded in
> your book.
> Every moment was laid out
> before a single day had passed
> (Psalm 139:16, NLT).

Every vacation destination has a history. Sometimes, that's what draws us to visit a specific place. We travel to the Holy Land to walk where Jesus walked. We fly to Normandy, France, because our grandfathers fought on its beaches. We visit Washington, D.C., so we can stand on the spot where Martin Luther King, Jr. gave his "I Have a Dream" speech.

Whether we have a personal connection to our vacation destination or not, that specific point on the globe doesn't exist in a vacuum. It has a story to tell. We hear echoes of its story in the statues, plaques, monuments, and museums located there. These make great photo ops. They also present us with another opportunity—they challenge us to put ourselves in someone else's shoes.

As we walk the halls of Anne Frank's house in Amsterdam, we imagine what it would have been like to have been a member of Anne's family, hiding from the Nazis. We ask ourselves if we'd be brave enough to hide a Jewish family in our home. Or perhaps we try on the boots of those who followed Hitler. How easily could we be swayed by charisma, peer pressure, and prejudice?

Through God's gift of imagination, we can develop a deeper sense of empathy with those whose lives were very different from our own. We can picture what it might have been like to be a slave picking cotton on a Southern plantation or a soldier forced to build a railway through the jungles of Thailand. We can mentally try on the shoes of both the privileged and the downtrodden.

The truth is we could have worn any of those shoes in real life. Where we were born, when, and to whom are foundational points in our own story. Points that are in God's hands, not our own. The more shoes we mentally try on, the greater appreciation we'll have for our own place in history—and the greater empathy and compassion we'll have for others.

Consider how your life story might differ if you had been born wherever you are visiting today.

Just Enough

> We are truly wealthy. We have a "profit" that is greater than theirs— our holy awe of God! To have merely our necessities is to have enough (1 Timothy 6:6, TPT).

There's a certain art to packing a suitcase, and not everyone is a natural-born artist. Some people wait until the last minute, then throw whatever is close at hand into their duffel bag. They figure if they have the bare essentials, they can buy or borrow anything else they need. These are the travelers most likely to arrive at their destination without a toothbrush or underwear.

Then there are the over-packers. Spontaneity is not their strong suit. They plan on being prepared for anything short of nuclear war. Along with packing twice as many clothes as they will ever use on vacation, their carry-on resembles a small pharmacy, complete with medications for cold, flu, allergies, bug bites, sunburn...you name it. Duct tape? Nail glue? Eyeglass repair kit? They have it.

Then, there are the "just enough" folks. They carefully consider where they are headed and put a lot of time and thought into what they will need. They pack with precision, using every square inch of their luggage to its best advantage. They rarely check their baggage, because they can usually fit everything into a carry-on bag—and still have room for a few souvenirs.

The way we pack for a vacation is a reflection of how we live at home. Some people just kind of mosey along, letting circumstances direct where they will go and what they'll do. Others worry about every detail of their days, including all of the valuable stuff they own. They cling tightly to their plans, afraid life will spin out of control if they don't.

Then, there are those who go through life content with "just enough." Even if their luggage were lost, they'd make do with what they had and still enjoy their vacation. They focus on what's truly important both at home and while they're away. They trust God, work hard, and enjoy every day God brings their way. What kind of packer are you?

Are you an under-packer, over-packer, or do you fall somewhere in between? Do you feel this characteristic is reflected in any other part of your life?

Exploring God's Gallery

"Stop and consider the wondrous works of God" (Job 37:14, ESV).

Paris, Barcelona, Istanbul, NYC: sometimes we travel to experience a slice of civilization that's unlike our own. Other times, we're drawn to solitary, uncivilized places. Destinations where the only art gallery is the great outdoors—each masterwork signed by the hand of God.

Man-made wonders like the Taj Mahal, Eiffel Tower, or Parthenon are all amazing in their own right, but for sheer awe, they simply can't compare to God's natural wonders of the Grand Canyon, the Great Barrier Reef, the Northern Lights, and so many more.

For those of us who know the artist personally, spending time in God's gallery can draw us closer to him. But even those who haven't yet made his acquaintance acknowledge that there's something powerful about nature. It invokes a sense of awe that bears a keen resemblance to worship even in those who aren't certain who or what they are worshipping.

Ralph Waldo Emerson wrote, "If the stars would appear one night in a thousand years, how would men believe and adore." This is true about all of God's creation. From the miracle of birth to the laws of gravity, the natural world is wonder piled upon wonder. We are so used to the daily miracles of a tree bearing fruit or a heart pumping blood that we don't give them much thought. It takes the sight of Mount Everest or a grove of giant sequoias to remind us how small we are and what a mysterious world we live in.

Let awe find a permanent home in your heart. Experience some of God's amazing creations firsthand. When your vacation is over, continue to nurture a sense of wonder and delight in creation. Even if you can't see the Grand Canyon every day, you can look in the mirror. The Bible tells us that's where God's greatest masterpiece can be found.

Spend some time outside today. How does thinking of nature as God's gallery change the way you look at a scenic view, a trip to the zoo, or your own reflection in the mirror?

Escape Artist

I say to myself, "If only I could fly
away from all of this!
If only I could run away to the place
of rest and peace.
I would run far away where no one
could find me,
Escaping to a wilderness retreat"
(Psalm 55:6-7, TPT).

In movies about space travel, there's always an escape
pod. If the mother ship is in trouble, the crew races to
the escape pod so they can disengage themselves from
whatever catastrophe is taking place on the ship. It's their
safety net and, hopefully, their safe passage home.

Is travel your escape pod? It's not an uncommon view.
When life is stressful, we long to leave our current
troubles behind and head somewhere far away:
somewhere those troubles can't follow us. There's nothing
wrong with that. It's important to take a break when life
is hard. It can help renew our energy and clear our head.

After all, a change of pace, and place, may be just what we need to gain a fresh perspective on what we want to escape from. It can jumpstart our creativity and problem-solving abilities. It may even help us come up with that solution we've been searching so hard to find.

However, our *escape* becomes counterproductive if our vacation is really a form of procrastination. When we put off important matters like dealing with debt, breaking an unhealthy habit, confronting a relational problem, or making that doctor's appointment we should have made months ago by telling ourselves, "I'll face that after I get back from vacation," we're not doing ourselves any favors. If we use our vacation as an excuse, chances are we'll find another excuse to use as soon as we get home.

Procrastination is never a good form of escape. It simply fills up our tomorrows with what we should accomplish today.

Don't drag the failing mother ship along with you on vacation. Disengage. But do it in a positive, productive way. Change *I'll face that after I get back from vacation* to *I'll finish that before I leave on vacation*. If you're already on vacation, set a due date for whatever it is you dread to face—big or small. Then, follow through. Do what you can, when you can, with what you have, and leave the rest in God's hands.

Consider the reasons you planned this vacation. If "escape" is one of them, ask yourself whether procrastination plays a part. If so, ask God to help you break this cycle and do what needs to be done.

Here Be Dragons

> When we obey him, every path he
> guides us on is fragrant with his
> loving-kindness and his truth (Psalm
> 25:10, TLB).

You Are Here. Those three little words matter a lot when
we're looking at a map. If we don't know where we are,
how can we figure out which direction we need to go to
reach where we want to be? When we're on vacation, a
map can point the way to our hotel or that pristine little
beach that's off the beaten track. And when the time
comes, a map can lead us home.

Luckily, accurate maps are readily accessible in this day
and age—many of them for free. But those maps came
at a price. Early explorers risked their lives to chart the
world. Without the benefit of modern transportation
and satellite photos, though, their maps were far from
complete. Entire sections of the globe were unexplored
and unrecorded.

A common misconception is that early cartographers labeled these uncharted areas with the warning, "Here Be Dragons." The truth is there's only one known map that contains these words: the Hunt–Lenox Globe. Built in 1510, this tiny copper globe now resides in the New York Public Library.

But there's a much older map, written over a span of 1500 years, that also warns us of dragons. When we venture off the grid of God's Word, we invite battles with proverbial, instead of mythical, beasts. We encounter fiery creatures like temptation, obsession, selfishness, and discontent. When we choose to move away from God, instead of toward him, we wind up in places we were never meant to go. These choices can not only change the course of our lives but the characteristics of our hearts. They can bring out the dragon in us.

It's so much wiser to stay on the path God has marked out for us. Instead of longitude and latitude, God provides commandments, instruction, history, poetry, and prophecy as navigational markers. They help us figure out our place in the world. They declare *You Are Here*. If drawing closer to God is our chosen destination, they'll help point us in that direction. One small step either direction can add up over time. Which direction will you choose today?

Review the choices you made yesterday. Do you think they moved you closer to or further away from God? How do you think your answer will influence today's choices?

_____

_____

_____

_____

_____

_____

_____

_____

_____

_____

_____

Dressed in God's Best

> Therefore, as God's chosen people, holy and dearly loved, clothe yourselves with compassion, kindness, humility, gentleness and patience (Colossians 3:12, NIV).

Suppose you were headed to Bermuda. You wouldn't pack snow boots or a winter parka. You also wouldn't fill your suitcase with clothes that weren't your size. Instead, you'd make certain that the garments you took were appropriate for your destination, for the activities you'd be participating in, and for the body God gave you.

God has another outfit he'd like you to take with you wherever you go. It's perfectly suited to every climate, culture, and activity you may encounter on your trip. It's also guaranteed to fit perfectly, even if you overindulge a bit at the breakfast buffet. It's always flattering on you—so much so that other people are bound to notice. It never wears out, gets soiled, or goes out of style. And believe it or not, it's free!

God asks all of his children to clothe themselves in qualities that reflect his personal style. Only then will they be fully dressed and ready for the day ahead. Attributes like compassion, kindness, humility, gentleness, and patience not only make you more beautiful inside and out, they attract those around you in a tangible way. People are naturally drawn to those who are kind-hearted, attentive, and generous of spirit.

The funny thing is that the more frequently you clothe yourself in God's couture, the more difficult it becomes to remove. Of course, why would you want to? Not only do other people see you in a more positive light, you'll begin to see yourself that way as well.

God's here to help you dress yourself in his best. But putting on his outfit isn't always easy. To achieve a perfect fit, God may have to strip you of other items you may have grown accustomed to wearing such as pride, selfishness, insecurity, and entitlement. Taking them off may be difficult, even painful, but the struggle is worth the final result. Being on God's best-dressed list is a wonderful place to be, whether at home or on the road.

Which one of God's garments (compassion, kindness, humility, gentleness, or patience) is the most difficult for you to wear consistently? How can you make it fit more comfortably in your life? Ask God to help you focus on that characteristic today.

Destination: Relationship

God places the lonely in families
(Psalm 68:6, NLT).

There is one destination in this world that outshines the rest. It's more valuable than England's crown jewels, more beautiful than Hawaii's fern grotto, more distinctive than Barcelona's La Sagrada Familia and more enduring than China's Great Wall. Its location is transient—and irrelevant. We'd travel to the ends of the earth and back just to spend one moment there. Regardless of how much time we spend, it's never, ever enough.

No exotic location could ever provide the joy we find in the presence of those we love. It's no wonder that so many vacation days are spent visiting friends and relatives. Whether it's a trip home for the holidays or a reunion with our closest friends, we long to connect with those we hold close at heart but who live far away.

Not that every moment we spend with friends and relatives is bliss. All too often we take those we love for granted. We fall back into familiar habits, nurse old grudges, or simply forget to cherish the limited time we have with each other. Perhaps that's just one more reason why we should not let too much time go by before we schedule our next rendezvous. We need to do what we can to ensure our family ties are not left in a knot.

Way back in Genesis, God proclaimed it was not good for man to be alone. His words still hold true today. God designed us for relationship; we are children created to love and be loved. Love can be tricky and messy, but it can also be the deepest, richest part of our lives.

When our vacation is centered around the people we love, what we do and where we go doesn't matter as much. So, let's make the most of the time we spend in the company of those we love. They are always worth the journey. Let's make certain they know that's true.

Today, think about those you're traveling with or those you've traveled to see. Do they know how much they mean to you? Tell them. Speak from your heart. Don't worry about being eloquent. Simply be sincere.

Vacation Envy

Peace of mind means a healthy body,
but jealousy will rot your bones
(Proverbs 14:30, NCV).

We're all familiar with the Ten Commandments. For those who love to travel, there's an Eleventh Commandment we often overlook. True, it's implied instead of carved in stone, but it's a temptation we face that's hard to resist. In fact, we've probably fallen prey to it over and over again. We may never covet our neighbor's spouse or our neighbor's goods, but coveting our neighbor's vacation... well, that's another story.

Vacation envy can strike at home or while we're on the road. We hear about a friend's upcoming trip to somewhere we could never afford to go. We have to decline an invitation for a reunion weekend because we can't get the time off work. We pass an amazing Five Star resort on the way to our budget motel. Even a travel brochure sent through the mail can leave us feeling envious of those who have the means to respond to the offer.

Envy makes our lives feel small. It shrivels up our gratitude and sucks the joy out of our own travel plans. So why allow it a foothold in our lives?

There's an effective way to flee this temptation. Compare down instead of up. There are many parts of the world where a vacation is a foreign concept. There is no time off work. No disposable income to spend on recreation and relaxation. No bucket list other than making it through another day. Even within our own communities, there are those who will never fly on a plane, sleep in a hotel, or travel far from where they were born.

If we have the ability to travel for pleasure, we are privileged—even if our lodgings are solely economy and our meals are ordered at a drive-thru window. Any vacation we take is a gift. Let's open it with gratitude and enjoy it to the fullest.

As you go about your traveling, sightseeing, eating, conversing, and basking in the adventure of today, ask God to help you be more aware of each privilege you enjoy. Then, remember to say, "Thanks."

Go to Grow

In all your ways acknowledge him,
and he will make straight your paths
(Proverbs 3:6, ESV).

When we think about opportunities for spiritual growth, Bible studies, church retreats, and Sunday morning services most readily come to mind. But God can use our vacation time just as easily as our quiet time to help us grow stronger, deeper, and more mature in our faith.

Vacation days provide the perfect petri dish in which faith can grow. We're more attuned to what's going on around us because we're removed from our routine. We have the opportunity to meet people outside of our usual circle of friends: people who may challenge us, teach us, or even become friends for life. We'll also undoubtedly experience situations that will put our patience, preconceived notions, and unconditional love to the test.

In other words, we'll have the opportunity to put into

practice what we've learned from all of those Bible studies and spiritual retreats.

Being stretched and challenged may not sound like the relaxing time we had planned. But growth doesn't take effort as much as it does attentiveness. The more aware we are of God's presence wherever we go, the more opportunities for growth we'll find open up to us along the way.

Of course, it's easy to become self-focused on vacation—to lose sight of God because we're so busy trying to treat ourselves. But he's always there, working behind the scenes, even if we get distracted. That's why it's so important to reconnect with him when we wake in the morning and before we fall asleep at night. His Spirit will help us see God's hand at work more clearly throughout the day, as well as those little green shoots of spiritual growth that are taking root in our heart.

A road trip to Damascus changed Saul of Tarsus' life. Who knows how God will use the trip you're on to change you.

Ask someone who knows you well how he or she has seen you grow in your faith this past year—or journal about how the trip you're on is affecting you spiritually.

An Outsider's Insight

God has given all people over to their stubborn ways so that he can show mercy to all (Romans 11: 32, NCV)

Never leaving home has its advantages. We know how to make life work at home. We know the language, the lay of the land, and where the closest bathroom is when we're in need. We know we can eat the food and drink the water without fear of compromising our intestinal health. Chances are we also have a personal group of cheerleaders nearby—a circle of friends who know us by name. They accept us, quirks and all. They know all about the job we hold, our marital status, our faith, our fears, and how we like our lattes.

But when we travel, we're the newbies. We don't *belong*. We're only visiting. If we've traveled to a distant country, the fact that we're foreigners may be readily apparent to those we meet. We don't understand the language, the currency, or the customs. Our appearance, and sometimes our clothes, may not blend in with the rest of the crowd. We may be treated as honored guests or unwelcome intruders.

Stepping into the role of foreigner is not always a comfortable one, but it provides us with a valuable education. It can help us understand what it feels like to be an outsider: a role many people step into every day. Whether they are new to the area, foreign immigrants, disenfranchised, or physically or mentally challenged, there will be always people who do not quite fit in. For them, where they live right now may never feel like a true home.

From God's point of view, there are no outsiders—only people he loves and wants to welcome into eternal life with him. As God's children, we can extend compassion and a warm greeting to others on his behalf. We can also recall how it feels to be on the outside. Then, we can put that experience to good use by doing for others what we needed others to do for us.

Is there any way in which you feel like an outsider today? How can you use this insight to help *outsiders* feel more welcome when you return home?

_____

_____

_____

_____

_____

_____

_____

_____

_____

_____

_____

_____

Road Trip

Pleasant words are like a honeycomb,
Sweetness to the soul and health to
the bones (Proverbs 16:24, NKJV).

With the completion of Route 66 in the summer of 1926,
the road trip was born. Kitschy motels, roadside diners,
and miles of open highway enticed travelers to drive from
Chicago all the way to the California coast. Though only
portions of the Mother Road remain, road trips are still
going strong. They're one of the most affordable kinds
of travel, especially for families. Spending long hours
together buckled into a moving vehicle gives new meaning
to the words *captive audience*.

In the heyday of Route 66, people spent most of their
time on the road enjoying the view out the window and
carrying on a conversation with their fellow travelers. Back
then, the idea that children would watch movies, play
video games, or wear headphones so they could listen to

their own music while parents talked on their phones as they drove, would have sounded like a space-age fantasy. That fantasy is our present-day reality. While it's true that the gadgets and gizmos we use on the road can help pass the time, they do nothing to draw a family closer together. And isn't that what a vacation is all about?

If your family is accustomed to focusing on electronics while on the road, come up with some fun ways to power down every once in a while. Playing license plate bingo, joining in a family sing-along, or having everyone answer questions like, "What's been the best day of your life so far?" or "If you could live anywhere in the world, where would it be?" sounds kind of corny. But it can help your family feel more connected when you arrive at your destination.

There will never come a day when we look back on a family vacation and lament, "I wish we'd spent more time playing video games." But there will come a time when we'll long for just one more moment with the ones we love. Making the most of the days God's given us doesn't mean finding new ways to entertain ourselves; it means finding new ways to love like he does.

Think of three questions that could open up an earnest discussion with your traveling companions. Then, find the right time to ask them—and listen carefully to what they have to say.

_____

_____

_____

_____

_____

_____

_____

_____

_____

_____

_____

Favorable Footprints

> The Lord God put the man in the
> garden of Eden to care for it and
> work it (Genesis 2:15, NCV).

Wherever we travel, we leave footprints. Some are a blessing; others are a curse. How big they are doesn't depend on the size of our shoe but on the size of our ego. While some may fade away in a relatively short span of time, the impact of others may continue for generations. All the while, we may be totally unaware of the impression we're leaving behind.

One kind of footprint we create affects the world around us environmentally. When we're at home, we may recycle, shun littering, try not to waste food, and drive an eco-friendly vehicle. These may feel like little things, but they add up. So do the efforts we make to care for our temporary home when we're visiting another part of the world. Using biodegradable sunscreen when we're swimming in the ocean or refraining from taking every free travel brochure that's available (then throwing most of them away, unread and unused) are just two little things we can do that make a big difference over time. God entrusted us with the care of this beautiful world. That's a responsibility we should take seriously anywhere we happen to be.

As visitors, we not only have an impact on the environment we visit but on the people who live there. Do we make choices that improve the lives of those we meet? Do we treat them with respect? Do we refuse to purchase items manufactured by child or slave labor? Do we steer clear of buying counterfeit name brand goods? Do we declare everything we've purchased on our customs form? Or do we try and sneak pink sand from Bermuda, cigars from Cuba, or items made of ivory from Africa back home with us?

As God's children, we want every footprint we leave behind to be one that others would benefit from following. We want to be goodwill ambassadors both for our home country and for our faith. We can't help but change the world by living in it. Why not change it for the better, one small step at a time?

Consider what you did and said yesterday. What kind of footprint did you leave?

The Bottomless Bucket List

All who are led by the Spirit of God
are sons of God (Romans 8:14, TLB).

Sometimes it feels like there's a hole in the bottom of our
bucket list. The more wonderful places we cross off the
list, the longer our list seems to grow. If we're fortunate
enough to spend a week in Maui, we feel the itch to
explore the other Hawaiian Islands as well. If we embark
on an anniversary cruise, every port we visit holds the
promise of so much more than we can see in one day.

Chances are we'll never empty our bucket of hopes and
dreams. The world is so big and life is so short. There'll
always be more places to go and things to do than we can
squeeze into one lifetime.

Sometimes we're forced to cross things off our list not
because life is too short but because circumstances have

changed. Finances, health concerns, political unrest in a part of the world we hoped to see...there are countless reasons why some of our travel dreams may not come true.

That's when it's time to dream a new dream. Consider what it is about a specific location or adventure that makes it so appealing. It's natural beauty? Architecture? Art? Outdoor activities? Culture? Cuisine? Ask God to help you discern the "whys" behind a long-dreamed-of locale. Then, brainstorm other options that carry a similar experience. If you're a bona fide Francophile but can't travel to France, why not visit the French Canadian city of Quebec? Dreaming of Denmark? Spend a weekend in Solvang (a little Danish town complete with windmills and *aebleskiver*) in central California. Need to stay closer to home? Travel vicariously through books and film.

Life is filled with twists and turns—and bucket lists that may never be fully realized. At least in this lifetime. But there's more to come. Along with a new body, Scripture tells us a new heaven and new earth are part of God's plan. There'll be no bucket lists because there'll be no bucket left to kick—just eternity stretched out before us with new worlds to explore. That sounds like a traveler's dream come true.

Write out your travel bucket list.
What draws you to these particular
destinations? Talk to God about
what's at the core of these longings.
Is there any other way to fill them?

Too Good to Be True

"This is how much God loved
the world—he gave his uniquely
conceived Son as a gift. So now
everyone who believes in him
will never perish but experience
everlasting life" (John 3:16, TPT).

It looks so official when it comes in the mail: two free tickets to the Bahamas with a five-night stay in a luxury resort. Just sign and return this certificate to book your dream vacation!

Everything sounds amazing, until you read the itty-bitty fine print at the bottom of the page which lists all kinds of rules and stipulations. The "free" tickets require $250 in taxes and handling fees. The resort you'll be staying at is nowhere near the beach and undergoing extensive renovations. And, by the way, your stay will require you to book the all-inclusive dining package for a mere $150 per person, per day. In the end, the deal is anything but a deal. It's a scam.

Whether it's on the internet, in the mail, or advertised on TV, there are plenty of bogus vacation packages that people get tricked into booking. They easily bring to mind that old adage, "If it sounds too good to be true, it probably is." But there's one life-changing exception to that rule: the grace of God.

Jesus sacrificed his life for us so that we could spend eternity with him. He paid for our rebellion, for the countless times we turned our backs on God and chose to live *our way*. There's no itty-bitty fine print, no hidden fees, or cancellation clauses. God's free gift is actually free.

It's hard to believe, but it's true. We're promised the ultimate eternal getaway, an authentic ticket to paradise. To accept our ticket, we simply acknowledge that Jesus is who he says he is (God) and we are who he says we are (sinners in need of grace). We can't pay for this gift with good deeds or forfeit it with bad choices. God's gift is ours to keep—no strings attached.

In the midst of your vacation excitement, take a few moments just to sit with God and bask in the goodness of his grace. Then, before you go to bed tonight, consider how your time with God influenced the rest of your day.

Savor the Here and Now

> This is the day the LORD has made;
> We will rejoice and be glad in it
> (Psalm 118:24, NKJV).

All great vacations must come to an end. And we're fully aware of what's waiting for us when we get home. A glut of unanswered email. A mountain of dirty laundry. A stack of unopened bills and junk mail. The challenge of getting back up to speed at work. Stepping on the scale to see how much weight we've gained while we were away. The same problems, conflicts, and struggles we were facing in life before we left are all still there, waiting for our return.

But we're not home yet. One of the biggest challenges we have as our vacation draws to a close is to prevent our minds from heading home before our bodies do. Whether we have a day, an afternoon, or even an hour of vacation left, let's not waste it. Why let tomorrow rob us of the pleasure and opportunities of today?

The often repeated Latin phrase *carpe diem* isn't found in the Bible. But it could be. The principle behind it echoes through verses that tell us not to worry about tomorrow (Matthew 6:34), to make the most of every opportunity (Colossians 4:5), and to remember that each day is made by the Lord. To "seize the day" means that we do what we can, with what we have, right here and now. On vacation, that may mean getting in one more round of golf, taking a nap in a hammock, or getting in the pool to play with our kids.

While *carpe diem* has become a modern day catch phrase, *carpe cras* has not. Sure, it doesn't sound as melodic, but more importantly, it can't be done. *Carpe cras* means "seize tomorrow." No matter how hard we try, we can't reach that far. Besides, none of us knows for certain what tomorrow will bring. Carrying the stress and worry of something that isn't here yet, or may never happen, can be amazingly taxing. Let's refuse to pick it up in the first place. Instead, let's grab hold of here and now and savor every moment.

Make a quick mental list of what's around you right now that you can't enjoy at home. Then, slow down and savor each one. When you return home: repeat. Savor what you missed!

Here's to Your Health

I pray that you may enjoy good health and that all may go well with you, even as your soul is getting along well (3 John 1:2, NIV).

When God created our world, he spoke into being an incredible place. Mountains, meadows, salt flats, and savannas...every spot on the globe is filled with wonder. But there is another world inside each of us: a living geography of muscles, blood vessels, bones, and more. Its intricacy, efficiency, and resiliency is mind-boggling. The more we explore it, the more even the most brilliant physicians and biologists are forced to admit that we still don't fully understand what makes us tick.

Going on vacation can be good for our overall health. A change of pace and place can help lower our stress levels and stimulate creative thinking. We can catch up on sleep, enjoy a bit of exercise, and feel free to laugh and play. But sometimes, our bodies don't seem to get the memo. We pick up an unwanted bug at the airport or our digestive system goes haywire when introduced to unfamiliar foods. Or perhaps it's something more serious—an illness or injury that sends us to the hospital. Maybe it even sends us home.

Regardless of what's gone wrong in our bodies, whether we have a chronic health problem we pack along with us wherever we go or we're struggling with an unexpected affliction, it's time to focus. Instead of focusing on what isn't working well, let's consider how incredible it is that all of those itty-bitty interconnected parts of us work happily together so much of the time.

The fact that our bodies have the ability to grow, to heal, and to help create other amazing humans beings is nothing short of miraculous. But, our bodies are also breakable and transient. So, if they demand a time out while we're on vacation, let's listen. They've been our main source of transportation since birth. Let's do what we can to keep them going strong.

What is one way you can treat your body well today? Do it. Consider it a thank-you note to God for his miraculous gift.

Curiosity Is the Key

"Do you know the mind and purposes
of God? Will long searching make
them known to you? Are you
qualified to judge the Almighty?
He is as faultless as heaven is
high—but who are you? His mind is
fathomless—what can you know in
comparison? His Spirit is broader
than the earth and wider than the
sea" (Job 11:7–9, TLB).

We've all seen them. Maybe, we've even traveled with
them. They're the tourists who ooze a certain smugness
that could be summarized as "Been there. Done that.
Have the t-shirt." They've accumulated plenty of frequent
flyer miles over the years, but they've misplaced their
sense of wonder somewhere along the way.

If you have the challenge of sharing a table with them at
dinner, just keep asking them questions about themselves

because it's fairly certain they'll never ask anything about you. As a matter of fact, they rarely ask questions at all. The feeling that they've seen it all has led them to believe they know it all. Nothing could be further from the truth.

The world is not a checklist of things to see and do that we can cross off in one lifetime. It's a curiosity shop, so filled with mysterious treasures that every time we take another look, we discover something new. The key is to stay curious. Keep asking questions, exploring new places, and being humbled by the fact that there's always more to learn.

That's not only true in regard to nature, culture, and every individual we encounter in this world, but also to our faith. It's okay to question God, Scripture, and long-held beliefs. God doesn't ask for blind faith. What he says is that we will "walk by faith, not by sight" (2 Corinthians 5:7, NKJV). That means we will keep moving toward him even if some of our questions go unanswered in this life.

Curiosity keeps us headed in the right direction—while keeping apathy at bay. If the visible world is so immense and complex that we can never fully comprehend it, surely the invisible world is even more so. Let's not become followers of Jesus who have an attitude toward our faith that says, "Been there. Prayed that. Memorized the verse." There's so much more to explore about our heavenly Father and the world he's created.

What question would you most like to ask God? Ask him. Listen for his answer in the coming days. Search the Scriptures. Ask those whose faith you respect for insight. If your question remains unanswered, ask God to help you rest in what you know to be true, humbly accepting the fact that you'll never comprehend it all.

Treat Yourself Well

> Whether you eat or drink or whatever you do, do it all for the glory of God (1 Corinthians 10:31, NIV).

As city mottos go, "What happens in Vegas, stays in Vegas" has proved exceedingly popular. What better safeguard could visitors ask for when their destination is nicknamed Sin City? Gambling, drinking, prostitution...these are the type of activities that have become synonymous with The Strip. But that doesn't mean we have to partake of any of them. There are lots of perfectly wonderful, God-pleasing things to do in Las Vegas.

The truth is any city, small town, or corner of the globe has the potential to become Sin City. It all depends on what we choose to do there. When we leave on vacation, we often have the mindset that it's time to treat ourselves. We don't plan on breaking all the rules, but we feel as though we have permission to at least bend them a bit. We set aside our diet, our budget, and sometimes our common sense. It may feel good for a while, but both experience and God's Spirit remind us that our decisions have consequences we'll regret further down the road.

Treating ourselves should mean treating ourselves right, not overindulging in things that will ultimately harm us. That's why God gave us his commandments in the first place. It wasn't to restrict our freedom and inhibit our fun. His commandments are meant to guide us into living a life of love that benefits us, as well as those around us. That includes our relationship with God. When we follow his rules, they lead us where we really want to go.

When we're on vacation, let's remember to treat ourselves well. That doesn't mean saying no to every dessert at the buffet table; it also doesn't mean eating *every* dessert at that table. It means finding a balance, enjoying ourselves in a way that would make God smile.

What areas are you tempted to overindulge in when on vacation? Ask God to help you treat yourself in a healthy, positive way in these areas.

Thanks for the Memories

I remember what happened long ago;
I consider everything you have done.
I think about all you have made
(Psalm 143:5, NCV).

It's been said that familiarity breeds contempt. Certainly that's more the exception than the rule. Familiarity can also give birth to friendship, comfort, relaxation, and many happy memories. It's one reason why some people travel to the same location year after year. The family cabin on the lake, that cozy hideaway where the staff knows you by name, the same beach where you spent your honeymoon…some spots on the globe beckon us back like a bird who's destined to migrate "home."

When it comes to vacation time, familiarity can be just as enjoyable as novelty. For some people, it's even preferable. Some of us find navigating the unknown incredibly stressful. When we visit our favorite restaurant, we order the same thing every time. We prefer what's tried and true over what's new. And forget about traveling anywhere that involves passports or a foreign language!

Choosing to use our free time in a way that refreshes our soul is a wise choice. Let's just be certain it's still a choice and not a habit. If what we used to enjoy by returning to a favorite spot now leaves us annoyed because of how things have changed over time, perhaps the vacation destination we're searching for can only be found in the past.

Happy memories are an irreplaceable gift. We can't recreate them even by going to the same location and doing the same things. We can still find great joy in the nostalgia of what's familiar, but we need to add to our store of memories and not try to survive on a life of reruns.

Go ahead. Return to your favorite place. But don't forget to pack a fresh point of view. Both you and your special spot can't help but change as time goes by. Consider in what ways you've both changed for the better. Then, find a way to celebrate your history, and your future, together. Make some new memories in your old stomping grounds.

If you had to return to one favorite spot year after year, where would it be? Consider why it's so special to you. Take time to thank God for the gift of happy memories.

Crowd Control

> Warn those who are lazy, comfort
> those who are frightened, take tender
> care of those who are weak, and be
> patient with everyone. See that no
> one pays back evil for evil, but always
> try to do good to each other and to
> everyone else
> (1 Thessalonians 5:14–15, TLB).

When we anticipate going on vacation, there's a part of
travel that none of us look forward to with fondness:
waiting. We wait in line for security at the airport, in traffic
along the road, and for a table at a restaurant when we
finally have time for a bite to eat. We wait to check in, to
check out, and to buy tickets for the sights we've come to
see. We even have to wait in line to use the bathroom.

Why do we wait? People. Lots of them. Crowds made
up of individuals just like us are all trying to make their
way through another day. It's easy to see crowds as an

obstacle when we're on vacation and forget that we are part of the whole. After all, to those behind us in line we are the ones in the way.

When God looks at the world, he doesn't see a horde of humanity. He sees individuals. And when he chose to make a personal appearance here on earth, Jesus presented himself to us as a person—one single, solitary individual. Just another face in the crowd. Although Jesus spoke to large crowds, he healed individually, attending to each person according to his or her specific needs.

When waiting for something or someone starts to raise our stress level on vacation, let's take another look around us. Let's focus on individual faces, instead of the length of the line in front of us. Every person in the crowd is a story being written one moment at a time. We have no idea what that story is, whether it's a tale of adventure or tragedy, love or loss. From our vantage point, all we can do is check out the book cover. Instead of making judgments, we can offer prayers. We don't need to know their names. God does. What better way to spend time in line than by touching the lives of those in it in a positive way?

Patience is a virtue that's useless unless it's put to the test. What has tested your patience the most on this trip?

Divine Treasure Hunt

Ever since the world was created,
people have seen the earth and sky.
Through everything God made,
they can clearly see his invisible
qualities—his eternal power and
divine nature. So they have no
excuse for not knowing God
(Romans 1:20, NLT).

What are we looking for when we're on vacation? Adventure? Beauty? Knowledge? Relaxation? Perhaps one of the things our heart is actually searching for is God. We're looking for evidence of his power in the ferocity of the sea, his tenderness in the delicate dance of the clouds, and a faint shadow of his image in the faces of those whose culture and life experience are literally a world apart from our own.

This isn't a futile search. Scripture tells us God has left divine fingerprints on everything he's made. God's world is like a treasure map pointing us right back to him. All we have to do is follow the clues. What can birdsong reveal about the playful nature of our God? What can the intricacy of an insect's wing tell us about his attention to detail? What can kindness from a stranger in a foreign country tell us about how God has fashioned the human heart?

When we're busy sightseeing, it's easy to overlook our invisible God in the midst of it all. But there's so much more to explore than what meets our eye. As we travel through the world God's made, one way for us to uncover more about the Creator's character is to invite him along. Asking God to join us on our journey helps make us more aware of his presence at every turn. Of course, he's always with us wherever we go, whether we invite him or not. But acknowledging him reminds us to look for signs of his power and clues to his character as we head out to partake of whatever adventure we've planned for the day.

Wherever today finds you, you're surrounded by God's handiwork. Every landscape, every wildflower, every face that you see can remind you of him—and provide a clue about the character of his divine nature. What will God reveal about himself to you today?

Think back to what you did yesterday. What evidence of God's hand can you find in the midst of it all?

Just Passing Through

"Your heart will be where your treasure is" (Luke 12:34, NCV).

It's tempting to want to lead a super-sized life. To get more for our money. To make certain every vacation is bigger and better than the one before. To buy a larger home and fill it with more stuff. To buy a more spacious fridge to keep more perishable food on hand. To chase a better paying job to pay for it all.

Perhaps it's more in line with Scripture to take a lesson from the travel aisle of our local drug store. There, everything is travel-sized. Sure, we spend more for less, but we don't buy more than we need. Everything is small, portable, and practical. There's just enough toothpaste, shampoo, or mouthwash for one trip.

When we travel, we know it's beneficial to pack light. We don't want to cart around more than we can carry. Heavy, cumbersome luggage gets in our way and slows us down.

It's also unnecessary. After all, on vacation it's not what we own or what we wear that matters. It's all about what we're going to see and do.

In the end, the same is true of life. It's what we do—how well we love—that matters. The more stuff we own, the more time, energy, and resources it takes for us to care for it all. That means we have less of life to spend on loving.

We're all just passing through in this life—travelers on the road to heaven. But all the stuff we pick up along the way is going to stay right here. It will either be thrown away, given away, or passed down to someone we love. By choosing to super-size our love and travel-size our possessions, we can make the most of the time we have here on earth and leave behind a legacy of incomparable worth.

Consider what's packed in your suitcase. What else do you really need to live? Think of one thing you can do to make your life less super-sized when you get home.

Go Ahead and Giggle

Those who go out weeping,
bearing the seed for sowing,
Shall come home with shouts of joy,
carrying their sheaves
(Psalm 126:6, NRSV).

Vacation is the perfect time to pray a very dangerous prayer. It goes something like this, "Lord, please help me never lose my sense of humor." Praying these words with sincerity of heart can be pretty risky because God's likely to answer it in ways that may put our patience, pride, and plans to the test. Consider yourself warned.

Then, go ahead and pray this prayer anyway because you know what's going to happen somewhere along the road. Your suitcase is going to take an unexpected trip around the world without you. The special Jacuzzi tub in your room is going to misfire, providing an unscheduled performance of dancing waters. The unpronounceable entree you order will be so spicy you'll cry harder than you did at your daughter's wedding. Or customer service will be so laughably lacking you'll find yourself searching for a hidden camera, certain you're being filmed for a reality show.

Regardless of the situation, getting giddy beats getting frustrated every time. It helps us see things from a more positive perspective. It also benefits us physically. Laughter boosts our energy, strengthens our immune system, releases endorphins, and reduces stress. It can even help prevent heart disease. That's one of the best workouts we can find without going anywhere near the gym. Laughter is also incredibly contagious, which means our light-heartedness benefits those around us.

Let's take our vacations, and ourselves, a little less seriously. This time we've set aside isn't a critical task we're required to accomplish. It's a gift to be opened leisurely and enjoyed. By asking God to help us keep our sense of humor close at hand throughout our holiday, we'll not only have a better time, we'll have more enjoyable stories to share with others when we return.

When on this trip have you needed a sense of humor? Was yours readily available?

Homeward Bound

Our citizenship is in heaven
(Philippians 3:20, NIV).

If our travels lead us across international borders, there's one thing we can't leave home without: our passport. It's our global ID. It not only lets the world know who we are, but to what country we pledge our allegiance—and our taxes.

We can be born into citizenship or acquire it via paperwork. The latter involves switching our allegiance from our native country to a newly chosen home. Regardless of what country our passport says we're from, God says our true citizenship lies beyond the boundaries of this world.

How does our citizenship in another world affect our life in this one? Well, our customs may seem a bit strange to those who are unfamiliar with our heavenly homeland. Living a life that focuses on forgiveness, unconditional love, and sacrifice may leave others scratching their heads. After all, making choices centered on giving instead of getting is a rather foreign concept in this world.

But, our *odd* behavior and priorities may ultimately inspire others to be *awed*. The peace and perspective we have access to as citizens of heaven is like the quintessential travel promo: "Follow me... I know the way to paradise!"

Of course, just because we're God's children doesn't mean we always act like it. Our poor choices can speak more loudly to those around us than our wise ones. And those choices don't just reflect badly on us. In the same way rude tourists in a foreign country leave those who live there with the impression that everyone from that country must be equally ill-mannered, our ungodly actions taint the world's picture of who God is and what it means to be a citizen of heaven.

As citizens of heavens, we need to remind ourselves we're not home yet. We're all just passing through. As foreigners in this foreign land, let's be exemplary visitors. Not only for the sake of those around us, but because that's one way of showing God how much we love him—and how grateful we are for the privilege of calling his home our own.

Brainstorm one thing you can do today as a citizen of heaven that will positively affect those around you. Then, do it!

A Circle of Blessing

Blessed is he who considers the poor
(Psalm 41:1, NKJV).

Travel can weave a crazy quilt of emotions inside us. Excitement, wonder, joy, curiosity, amusement, awe...to name just a few. But the one that should overwhelm us again and again is gratitude. What a privilege it is to be wherever we find ourselves today!

Just taking a vacation is a foreign concept to many people around the globe. That's because for them there's no such thing as disposable income. Almost half of the world's population lives on less than $2.50 per day. That means necessities such as food, water, and shelter are not a given. As for education, sanitation, and health care, these can be considered a luxury. For many people, each and every day is a struggle for survival.

Now think about us. If we're on vacation, we've have more than enough to pay for necessities. We have enough to pay to play. This isn't intended to make us feel guilty, but grateful. Gratitude is more than a feeling though. It can also be a word or action—an outward expression of our heartfelt appreciation.

Let's do more than count our blessings. Let's make our blessings count. The more we take time to celebrate the gifts we've been given, the more grateful we'll feel. The more grateful we feel, the more frequently we'll express our thanks to God in prayer. The more we pray, the more easily we'll recognize God's voice as he prompts us to share the gifts he's given us with the world around us.

We can never repay God for all he's given us spiritually and materially. But we can pay it forward. We can take a percentage of our annual vacation budget and donate it to a charity that works in the area we're traveling to. We can fast one day—or even one meal—on vacation and give the money we save to feed a local family in need. With a bit of creativity, we can use our blessings to help bless the world.

Prayer is always a great place for action to begin. Ask God to help you come up with one way you can bless the poor wherever you are right now.

A Walk in the Park

"Take your sandals off your feet, for
the place on which you are standing
is holy ground" (Exodus 3:5, ESV).

Gardens are an important location in Scripture. The
Garden of Eden was man's first home. Gethsemane was
where Jesus went to prepare his heart for his ultimate
sacrifice. Furthermore, many of Jesus' parables center on
plants, seeds, and growth. Perhaps that's because there's
something about the verdant beauty of green, growing
things that feels both wild and holy at the very same time.
It feels a bit like God really is right here in our midst.

Whether your current journey has led you to the city or
the country, it's beneficial to find a leafy retreat to enjoy
while you're on the road. A botanical garden, a city park,
a forest path, or even a bench by a curbside flower bed
can all provide a wonderful opportunity for a quick "time
out." Even on vacation, we need them—those tranquil

moments when we slow down our pace, quiet our hearts, and regroup. They help remind us that we're not alone.

Though the days of Genesis are far behind us, God still walks through the garden with his children. Will we take time to notice he's there? It seems kind of silly to have to remind ourselves to slow down on our own vacation. Isn't that what vacation time is for? Yet, we often pack so much fun into so little time that we return home exhausted, instead of refreshed.

Why not let gardens become a kind of transcendent touchstone—a reminder that we truly are standing on holy ground everywhere we go? We may never see a burning bush in Central Park, but we may become more aware of God's whisper when the wind blows through the trees over our heads, or of God's loving care for all he's made when we delight in a blanket of wildflowers beneath our feet. The more aware we are of God's presence with us at all times, the more tempted we may be to take off our shoes.

God is with you, right here, right now.
What difference does that truth make
in your vacation? Let the next garden
you see help remind you he is near.

Detours, Dead Ends, and Delays

"See I am laying in Zion a stone that
will make people stumble, a rock that
will make them fall,
and whoever believes in him will not
be put to shame"
(Romans 9:33, NRSV).

One minute your anticipation and expectations are high.
The next they're deflated like a proverbial balloon. The
plane has mechanical difficulties. You misplace your credit
card. Your reservations from months ago disappear into
cyberspace. The Norovirus breaks out on your honeymoon
cruise. Your worst travel fears become reality.

Even the most careful travel planning can't keep the
unexpected at bay. But we can't always tell the difference
between catastrophe and serendipity. At least, not by
looking at our circumstances. Consider the Bible. Joseph

is attacked by his brothers, and then sold into slavery. A teenage girl named Mary gets pregnant out of wedlock. (Did I mention she's a virgin?) Jesus, our hero, dies! Sometimes, what looks like disaster proves to be an unconventional door to redemption.

We never know how a story, including the story of our lives (and even our vacation), turns out until we get to the end. And we're not there yet. In the meantime, what we *do* know is this: "We know that for those who love God all things work together for good" (Romans 8:28, ESV).

So, let's not panic. Instead, let's pray for perspective, perseverance, and a positive attitude. By tomorrow, once we've moved a bit farther down the road emotionally from whatever we're facing right now, we may realize that what felt like a disaster is simply an inconvenience. We like our plans to go our way. What better reminder for us that we're not in control than to have our perfectly laid plans go a bit awry.

God is at work in this world, weaving what may look like disaster into the fabric of our lives. We may never know if that delay on the highway saved us from crossing paths with a drunk driver—or if it simply became a much needed lesson in patience. It doesn't really matter. Either way, it was *good*.

What's the biggest disaster you've faced in your life? Name a few ways God worked things together for good through what you experienced. If you can't see the good, ask him to help you.

Healed and Whole

Lift your drooping hands and
strengthen your weak knees, and
make straight paths for your feet,
so that what is lame may not be put
out of joint but rather be healed
(Hebrews 12:12–13, ESV).

We can all use a place of healing in our life. Perhaps
it's our hearts—broken or bruised—that need room
to recover. It could be our minds—overworked and
overwrought—battling with worry, negativity, or the
overall perplexity of living in a fallen world. It may be our
bodies—exhausted, stressed, or dealing with a chronic
medical condition. It could be all three. Or more.

We all need an oasis where we can kick off our shoes,
relax, reflect, and recover from the rigors of ordinary,
everyday life. But we need this kind of safe harbor even
more desperately when life feels far from ordinary. Grief,
loss, a significant life change…when major stressors enter

our lives, they can wreak havoc with our sense of self and peace of mind.

If recuperation, more than recreation, is needed during your time away, it's in your best interest to simplify. Cut down on as many travel-induced stressors as possible. If flying stresses you out, drive—or revise your destination. If trying to squeeze everything you need for ten days into one carry-on leaves you pulling your hair out by the roots, check a bag: even if it costs a bit more. Let balance, instead of emotion, help you plan your meals. Don't schedule anything early in the morning so you can sleep in. And if you wake up one morning and what's on the day's agenda sounds overwhelming, exercise your right to say no. You can choose to take a day off—even on vacation! Being proactive isn't selfish. It's wise.

God longs for us to be healed and whole; we can tell by reading the gospels. Jesus treated those who were grieving, or dealing with physical or mental illness, with compassion. He didn't leave them the way he found them. He administered healing through a variety of different ways. In our lives, the right vacation at just the right time may be one of them.

What kind of healing do you need in your life? Ask God to help you use your current location as an oasis—a place of hope, refreshment, and recovery.

Giving on the Go

We should love people not only with
words and talk, but by our actions
and true caring (1 John 3:18, NCV).

What word do we use to describe the picture-perfect
vacation? *Paradise*. That cruise of the Greek Isles, the
all-inclusive beach resort and spa, even a tent pitched in a
pristine section of the woods (where we're close to nature
and far from people), can feel like it almost lives up to the
image we have of that word. But this world isn't paradise.
At least not in the Biblical sense.

No matter how ideal our holiday, there's no spot we can
travel to on this earth that remains unblemished. War,
poverty, disease, corruption, pollution, abuse...we humans
seem to be inexhaustibly creative when it comes to
finding new ways to hurt ourselves and each other. This, in
turn, hurts God. As every parent knows, you can't help but
ache when you see your children doing something that's
going to spell disaster for them down the road.

This truth isn't meant to be a killjoy: a wet blanket on the bonfire of our beautiful holiday. It's just a tiny little wake-up call. Not everyone gets to enjoy a bit of paradise here on earth by taking a vacation. If we're fortunate enough to be one of the few who do, why not change a bit of our free time from *me time* to *we time* by helping make a positive difference for others in God's world.

There are so many ways we can turn our empathy into action. Sign up for a short-term mission trip with a church. Help out at a state park. Offer to spend vacation time helping a service organization build homes, provide fresh water, or bring medical care to impoverished areas. Volunteer to do whatever needs to be done after a natural disaster.

One pair of hands and a willing heart can change the world—at least one tiny corner of it. That corner, whether it's around the world or across the tracks from where we live, is someone else's home: someone God loves. Making someone else's home feel a little bit more like paradise may turn out to be the best vacation we've ever had.

How does taking a volunteer vacation sound to you? Brainstorm what this might look like for you in the future.

What's Your Status?

Like cold water to a weary soul
is good news from a distant land
(Proverbs 25:25, NIV).

There was a time when postcards were all the rage. We wouldn't dream of going on vacation and forget to send one to friends and family. But that was then. Social media is now. Why bother purchasing someone else's picture and sending it via snail mail when we can post a personal photo that can instantly be seen by our large crowd of adoring fans? Wait...that's supposed to read *friends and family*. Or is it?

Social media is more than a scrapbook. It's kind of like having our very own paparazzi. They follow us everywhere. See what we're eating. Critique what we choose to wear to the beach. Envy our view from our hotel room. Know when we're out of town and when we're home—which is why it's wise to only include on our account "friends" we actually know. And trust. And that don't have a criminal record or a problem with kleptomania.

Other than the whole privacy and security debate, there's another debate we should have with ourselves when we travel. How much time should we spend with people who are not actually on vacation with us? If we refuse to stay anywhere that's not internet accessible, and we spend every free moment posting a play-by-play record of our day, perhaps we need to rethink why we're doing what we're doing.

Sure, there are folks back home who get honest joy out of vicariously traveling with us. But is that what's really motivating us? Or are we driven by a need to be "liked"? If the number of likes or comments on a post can make or break our day, we seriously need to unplug. It's a status symbol that's feeding a desire for approval and recognition.

Keeping in touch with friends is great. Social media can help us do that in an incredibly convenient way. But ultimately, it's God's approval, not our social media fans, that really matters. Whether we're home, or somewhere else around the world, we can rest in the fact that God "likes" us just the way we are.

Kick it old school on this vacation.
Send postcards, instead of posts, to
those you hold close to your heart
wherever you go.

Lost Baggage

"I am leaving you with a gift—peace of
mind and heart. And the peace I give
is a gift the world cannot give.
So don't be troubled or afraid"
(John 14:27, NLT).

You've made it to your vacation destination and you're
looking forward to having a marvelous time. Soon. But
right now, you're at the airport waiting for your bags.
Patiently. Then, not so patiently. Finally, the buzzer
sounds, the red light comes on and the conveyer belt
starts going around and around. One black bag after
another rolls by. You eye each one carefully, searching for
the one you know is yours. You'd recognize it in an instant.
After all, you've been carrying it around for years. But your
baggage is nowhere to be seen.

Instead of panicking, and picturing yourself wearing
the exact same outfit every day for your entire trip, you
rejoice. You throw your hands up in the air, high-five the

closest fellow passenger and shout, "It's finally gone!" That's not the usual reaction to lost luggage. Unless the baggage you've been toting around is emotional.

There's no better time to lose that matched set of emotional baggage than on the road. The novelty of travel has the power to jog our mind out of its usual rut. When we leave deadlines, To-Do lists, and the immediacy of our regular routine behind us, our minds have a chance to wander. Frequently they lead us back to underlying struggles often masked by the busyness of everyday life.

Grudges, regrets, negative words, emotional wounds... unless we consciously choose to let go of them, we can wind up toting them around for years. Not only do they weigh us down mentally, spiritually, and emotionally, they're also incredibly unattractive. Like a tattered suitcase poorly held together with duct tape, our personal baggage can leave a trail of dirty laundry wherever we go.

What's done is done. We can't change the past. But we can lighten our load for the future. With God's help, forgiveness, healing, and peace of mind are within reach. Sometimes, it may take a while to wrestle that baggage out of our hand—and heart. But why wait any longer to begin? What a treat it would be to arrive home lighter than when we left.

Every time you pick up your suitcase on this trip, do a mental baggage check. Is there anything you're carrying around emotionally that would be better left behind? Don't return home without taking one positive step toward letting go of what God never meant for you to carry.

_____

_____

_____

_____

_____

_____

_____

_____

_____

Pilgrim with a Purpose

> Blessed are those whose strength is in you,
> whose hearts are set on pilgrimage
> (Psalm 84:5, NIV).

Every year, over 100,000 people walk all or part of an arduous 450-mile trek between the French Pyrenees and Santiago de Compostela, Spain. They travel by foot over steep mountains, past isolated villages, and through major cities. But it isn't the magnificent scenery, historically significant landmarks, or exemplary architecture that draws people to set off on this pilgrimage known as "The Way of St. James." It's their relationship with God.

Maybe this sounds like fun; maybe it sounds like torture. Either way, we don't have to travel to a distant country to participate in a pilgrimage like this. By definition, a pilgrimage is a spiritual journey to a sacred place. If all the world is sacred, because there's not a corner where God's presence isn't found, then any journey can be a pilgrimage and every traveler a pilgrim. What matters is our heart, not our method of transportation or our location on the map.

If you long to draw closer to God right now, the journey you're currently on can be considered a pilgrimage. The only way to know if you've arrived at your destination is to have a specific objective in mind. How would you like to draw closer to God? What are some measurable goals you can use as landmarks?

It's up to you to plot your course. Perhaps you want to schedule in time each day to reflect on a specific verse of Scripture. Maybe you want to show God's love to those around you in concrete ways. You could even be so bold as to ask God to reveal an area in your life that needs to change—then act on what you hear.

Let's become pilgrims with a purpose, whether at home or on the road. In our daily walk with God there's always room for us to draw closer to his side.

How does referring to this trip as a spiritual pilgrimage change the way you look at it? Does it make your time away sound more, or less, appealing? Journal or pray about your response.

Coming Home

You see me when I travel
and when I rest at home.
You know everything I do
(Psalm 139:3, NLT).

Home. There's so much emotion packed into that one
little word. It's our destination at the end of every
vacation. It's the place we know well, as well as the place
we are known. Even when a vacation seems too short,
and we don't feel ready to head back home quite yet,
there's still a singular comfort waiting for us the minute
we walk through those doors. We drop our bags, kick off
our shoes, and settle back into our special corner of the
world—the place where we belong.

Travel can challenge and delight us. It can open our eyes,
stretch our minds, and charm our hearts. But it can also
make us appreciate the quiet pleasures of home. Our
own bed, our own street, our own familiar cadence to

the rhythm of life. Being gone for a while can remind us of what we've left behind. Absence *can* make our hearts grow fonder or, at the very least, more aware of what we may easily take for granted the rest of the year.

Unless we learn to cherish *home* and the beauty of an ordinary day, we may wind up believing that the best part of life is our next big trip to somewhere else. If we do, we'll miss what's right in front of us: the adventure waiting at our own front door.

We need to live wherever we are right now. That means when we're on vacation, we savor every minute. See the sights. Sample the cuisine. Revel in the grandeur of an unfamiliar landscape. But when we're home, we need to be all there. Do the job before us to the best of our ability. Delight in every unexpected joy God brings our way. Love God with our heart, soul, mind, and strength and our neighbors as ourselves. Be grateful for the blessing of being able to travel the world—and the blessing of coming home.

List at least ten things you love about being home. Keep them inside your Bible, travel devotional, or passport. Review them each time you're headed home from a trip.

_____

_____

_____

_____

_____

_____

_____

_____

_____

_____

The End

Let all that I am praise the LORD;
may I never forget the good things he
does for me (Psalm 103:2, NLT).

All vacations—and travel devotionals—must come to an end. When they do, it's time to look back on where we've been. What can we learn about ourselves, our world, and our God from the highs and lows and everything in between?

Reflecting on where we've been is a bit like glancing in our car's rearview mirror. We can't spend too much time with our eyes fixed on what's behind us or we'll never get where we're going. Granted, it can be difficult to stop looking back when we're leaving people and places we love behind. But life is a journey that keeps moving forward.

That being said, a glance back now and then helps us gain perspective. When we're driving, it provides the information we need to help us safely change lanes or assess our place in the flow of traffic. When we're reminiscing, it helps us discern our place in God's world and what we hope to change about ourselves and our future. It clues us in as to what we like or dislike. Our strengths and weaknesses. The evidence we've seen of our invisible God.

This is important because we have such short memories. Just like the Israelites who saw God part the Red Sea, then soon afterward doubted he could provide food and water in the desert on the other side, we quickly forget how we've seen God's power at work in our lives. When we take time to recall how God has come through for us, we'll be more prepared to face whatever lies ahead of us on the road of life.

When panic hits, we'll recollect how God provided a place of peace through prayer in the past. When doubt sets in, we'll recall how God changed our hearts, or our actions, in ways nothing else ever could. When we feel alone, we'll remember how close God's presence has been at other times in our lives.

Wherever we go, we go with God. May every journey you take, and memory you make, help you become more aware of his power, his presence, and his love.